what am i

dave galey

what am i

Published by Winlock Publishing Co.
26135 Murrieta Rd.
Sun City, Ca 92585
(951)943-0014

Copyright © 2011 by Dave Galey

ISBN 9781890461-74-4

Library of Congress Catalog number 2005929703

Cover design and Illustrations: Dave Galey

Price: $15.95

i dont know what i am
i dont know what words are but i will play
like i do so i can tell my story

this may be hard to read because i dont
know how to capitalize and punctuate
(whatever that is)

**i was in a nice warm place and was jiggled
once in a while when all of a sudden i was
squeezed and mashed and and squashed and
slid out into the cold**

where am i. . .

**then i felt a warm slippery thing moving all
over me
it felt good**

**now i got the empty feeling and rooted
around until i smelled something and found
this squashy thing to suck on and my
tummy started feeling better**

it is still dark but i dont know what dark is

so it is ok
i fell asleep

when i woke up i had that empty feeling
again

i dont move too good but i kept wiggling
and squirming and smelling until if found
that squashy thing again and began to suck
on it

boy . . . that sure tastes good

i love that squashy thing but there are some
squirmey and wigglely things trying to
push me out of the way

sometimes those other things make me lose
that squashy thing but sometimes i get it by
pushing them away

so i sleep and suck and squirm and push
and sometimes i wobble and lose my way
and wobble around and sniff until i feel one
of those pushy things and they are warm

and wobblely and we manage to ⬚nd that
wonderful squashy thing again

a squashy thing for each of us
my life is slurp wobble sleep . . . slurp
wobble sleep . . . Slurp wobble sleep. . .
slurp wobble sleep

i woke up looking for that squashy thing
and a funny thing is happening

the dark is going away
things are growing light and lumpy

fuzzy shapes are showing up
those things that were pushing me away
look like me

there is that great big thing with the
squishy things that look like a giant me

that is where those warm slippery feeling
were coming from

i love that great big thing with the squishy
things

i think i will think of it as my momma

i love my momma

my momma is furry and soft and has lots of those squishy tasty things and i like it when she runs that warm slippery thing over me

i later learn that warm wet slippery thing is a tongue and i have one too

i am learning to use it on me and it is fun those other things that look like me keep pushing against each other and trying to get

at the squashy things

i think i will think of them as litter mates

there are ◻ve of them but i cant count so i
just think of them as more than one

i am getting so i can crawl wobble ◻ op and
crawl some more

a monster thing picked me up and it was smooth and not furry so i knew it was not my momma

it is kind of scary since this monster thing held me way up above my momma and litter mates and said coo-coo little puppy

it nuzzled me and made me feel good and that took the scare away and it kept calling me puppy

i like the sound of puppy
it sounds cuddlely and lovable so i guess i will call myself puppy

it is not too long after slurping crawling
and sleeping that i heard that monster thing
call some of my litter mates puppy too

being a very canny type of whatever
i have decided that we are all puppies and
one momma

so now all we puppies do is slurp sleep
crawl and we have invented a new game
we wrassle with each other

and we have more monster things come and
pick us up and say goo-goo or coo-coo or
chootchy chootchy coo
i dont know what this language is but the
monster things giggle and smile when they
do it

i must be getting real smart since i learned
today that one of the monster things is a
kathy and another is a brian

there are also some smaller monster things
called danny and suzzy and kiddy or maybe
it is kitty or something that sounds like
that

the kathy and the other monster things call momma moppet so i guess everyone has two names like momma and moppet

the kathy things is also called mommy and sweety and several other thinks i cant remember

the monster things are also called people

i know now that i am puppy but the people things are starting to call me whizbang

it is beginning to dawn on me that there are
things and there are names these things are
called so you can tell one from another

so i guess i will be called whizbang and that
is my name
moppet is my mommas name

gee i am getting smart
after a while that smooth people thing
called kathy starts putting something in
our nest

it picks up whatever that is and pushes it
into our mouths
it taste different but kind of good

i dont think it will replace that squashy
things

but momma keeps getting up and taking
those squashy things with her

momma has stayed away so long that my
mates and i try eating that stuff that kathy
left here

it is ok but it will never replace mommas
stuff

momma has been staying away so long we
are getting used to eating that other stuff

next thing we know there is some hard
stuff to eat

it is ok though because we are growing
hard little thing in our mouth that we can
crunch with

it is getting fun to wrassle and try to
crunch that wiggley thing at the end of my
mates and also that ⬚oppy thing on each
side of of their fronts

also our little stubby crawly legs are getting
long and strong enough to bounce and jump
and romp all over

every day or so a people thing picks one of
us up and smoozes and goo-goos over one of
us

i heard one girl people while she was letting

me slurp her say i will take this one and call
him waggles

hey . . .my name is whizbang and that is all i
will answer to

and what does it mean to take me

is take me a good thing
this girl people is named sally and sally says
my name is waggles

well i dont care what she call me as long as i
get something for my tummy

then sally puts me into a little box and
takes me out into a nest that moves

i leave all my mates and my momma and
wonder what is happening to me

the nest with the box with me moves and
shakes and swerves and ⊠nally it quits
moving and sally takes the box i am in into
another nest that does not move

sally makes a neat little bed for me and
shows me to a little people she calls bree

bree squeals and picks me up and squashes
me and then drops me and i cry a little

sally tells bree to be gentle that i am a little
puppy and my name is waggles

bree then smooths my fur and coo coos to
me

i then lick brees face and she giggles

sally has put out a dish with hard
cruncheys and wet stuff i heard them call
water

i slurp it up and it is good
then i go to sleep

i wake up and squat and pee

sally paddles my bottom and puts me on
paper with a lots of words on it

(i dont know what words are but i learned
later)

i think sally was mad at me for peeing

what else is a guy to do
anyhow every time i start to pee sally picks
me up and puts me on the word paper

being the very smart type i am

i figure that is where i am supposed to pee

so each time i pee there sally smiles and
gives me a little treat

now i gotta go poo poo so i go behind my
bed and poop

sally starts all over with the paddling and
puts me on the wordy paper

am i supposed to poo poo where i pee

i guess i am

the next day the wordy pee pee paper is
farther from my bed

so i think i am supposed to pee there
so i go farther to the wordy pee and poop
paper to pee

sally gives me a treat

it gets dark and gets light again and i go to
pee
the pee and poop paper is farther away yet

it is next to the big board that lets you in or
out of the big box
so i go to it and pee and poop

it gets dark and gets light again and i go to
pee

i cant find the pee & poop paper

then i see it through that part that lets light
in of the big board that lets you in and out
of the big box

i scratch at the big board cause i know sally
wants me to go on the paper

sally opens the big board she calls a door
this lets me out of the big box she calls the
house

i go to the paper and pee

sally gives me a treat

i am happy

sally tells me i am outside

now i am confused

am i puppy
am i whiz bang

am i waggles
am i outside

i guess i will think
about what i am
later

i am outside and it
is big

it is bigger than
the room i sleep in

it has a lot of big
brown things that
have a lot of hair at the top

i look at the big brown things with lots of
green hair at the top and sally tells me i can
pee at the bottom of them

later i learned that they are called trees and
they dont move or anything

they just stand there waiting for me to pee

on them

they dont even mind
sometimes i go behind them and poop and
they still dont care

sally got me a squeaky thing
it is fun

i wiggle at it and play like I am going to bite
it and toss it in the air

sally makes a happy noise when I do that

i like to hear sally make a happy noise

so i am living with sally and bree and
another people person that sally calls ben

ben is bigger than sally and sally is bigger
than bree but both ben and bree do what
sally tells them

so i guess sally is the boss

ben is not around the house most of the day
but when he comes home he picks bree up

and squashes her and she squeals and

then he puts his head against sally and they lick each other.

i know what i think . . I think sally is the momma person and bree is like a litter person.
i dont know what a ben is except he is a bigger person with a deeper sound

somedays bree will take me outside and play with me

bree chases me and then i chase bree and she squeals and falls down and make a lot of happy noise and i come over to her and lick her face and she squashes me and it feel good

every time it gets dark and then light again sally has put a bowl of food and a bowl of water for me to eat and lap.
sometimes i am not wanting to eat

when this happens sally gets upset and trries to put food in my face i just turn around and act like sally is not there

sometimes sally will put a good tasting thing she calls a treat in front of me

it is like when she was putting the pee pee paper down and i would pee on it and she would give me a treat thing

but even the treat did not make me want to eat so i just turned around and decided to sleep

one day sally picked me up and put me in that big box that moves and swerves

we were moving and bouncing and then we became still

sally picked me up and took me into a big room with a lot of other litter things

some were barking and some were just sitting there and some were making mean sounds

after a while i was
put on a shiny table
and a big person with
a white covering
started to squeeze
and pinch me.

then the big person
got some pointy
things and pushed
them into me and i
cried but not for long
then i heard the big
person in the white
covering say that i
am inoculated

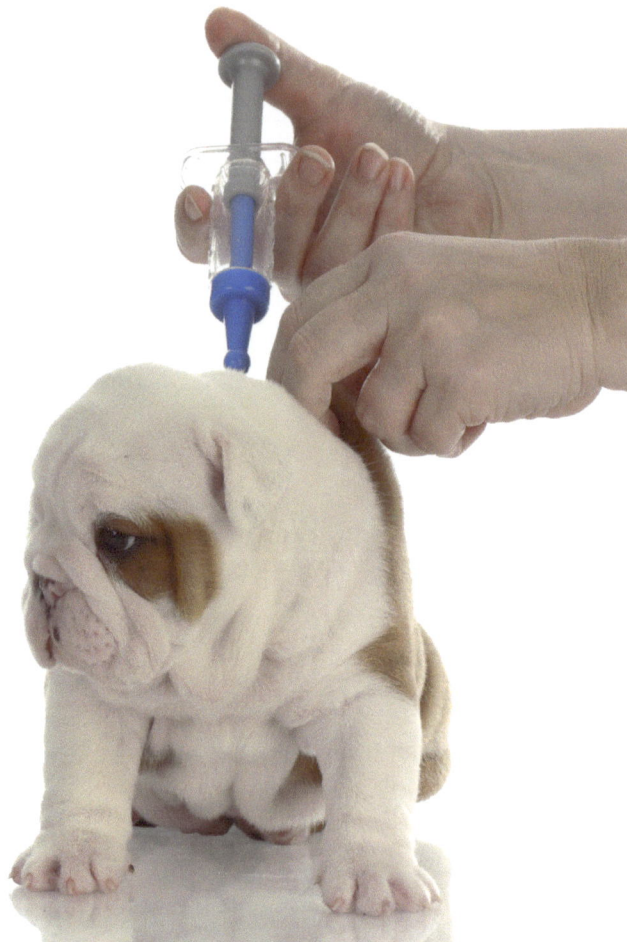

that really confuses me

am i puppy
am i whiz bang
am i waggles
am i outside
am i inoculated

i will have to think about that later

WHAT DO YOU THINK I AM

?

Dave Galey